PREDICTIONS

Warfare

FRANÇOIS HEISBOURG

PHŒNIX

A PHOENIX PAPERBACK

First published in Great Britain in 1997 by
Phoenix, a division of the Orion Publishing Group Ltd
Orion House
5 Upper Saint Martin's Lane
London, WC2H 9EA

A CIP catalogue record for this book is available
from the British Library.

ISBN 0 297 81848 1

Typeset by SetSystems Ltd, Saffron Walden
Set in 9/13.5 Stone Serif
Printed in Great Britain by
Clays Ltd, St Ives plc.

Contents

Introduction   1

1   **From Machetes to Designer-Genes:**
    The Tools of War   3

2   **The Devil's Playground**   16

3   **Grunts, Geeks and Crazies**   34

Conclusion   46

Further Reading   55

Introduction
War as a Social Activity

In attempting to predict the future of warfare, one needs to concentrate on why and by whom wars will be fought, and what kinds of wars they will be. The way technology is integrated into future conflicts will largely depend on the objectives of wars to come. Taking a comparison from society as a whole, it was easy twenty years ago to describe what fax machines and personal computers were supposed to do technically and how; but it was considerably more difficult – and much more important – to forecast their immense social impact. Similarly, a distinction must be made between the existence of technologies for warfare and their actual integration into combat.

We are witnessing a simultaneous transformation of the reasons for war and the means of war. The death of the totalitarian ideologies which accompanied the Industrial Revolution; the disappearance of the Soviet Empire; the undermining of the traditional role of the nation-state as the sole coiner of currency and organizer of military force; the emergence of a broad range of transnational centres of power and influence, from global financial markets to international criminal groups; the rebirth of tribal warfare, not least in the ex-communist states – all these are trans-forming the nature of warfare.

As for the tools of war, these are diversifying in striking ways which are already made obvious by what we see on our television screens. At one extreme, the Gulf War of 1990–1 highlighted video-arcade technology. At the other, primitive machetes killed more people in Liberia and

Rwanda than smart munitions ever did in the Gulf. Low-tech landmines kill and maim thousands of civilians long after their military utility has disappeared. But even in such cases modern technology is exploited to maximize the damage inflicted by the simplest weapons: the genocidal civil war in Rwanda was orchestrated by the electronic tom-tom of Radio Mille Collines, which directed the hands of the murderers in the remotest mountain hamlets. This synergy between the old and the new will be enhanced wherever the strategic pressures which weigh upon the Western democracies do not prevail. Limiting damage to innocent bystanders has not exactly been the dominant concern of the warlords in Bosnia of 1992–5, for whom driving out, or exterminating, 'ethnically' alien civilians has been a war aim in itself.

Finally, new technology opens up new battlefields, whose very existence was hardly conceivable only twenty years ago. American defence and intelligence professionals increasingly express their fears of an electronic 'Pearl Harbor', meaning a sneak attack against their computer networks by foes whose offensive capabilities in this domain have been direly underestimated. The first skirmishes of cyberwars waged by a vanguard of computer hackers have already occurred, even as hapless civilians were being chopped to death by age-old weapons in Monrovia or Kigali. Such contrasts will become the norm as universally available technologies are harnessed to vastly different military ends in contrasting social contexts.

Chapter 1
From Machetes to Designer-Genes:
The Tools of War

A three-dimensional conventional war rages on a global scale. Cruise missiles rain destruction on a territory the size of the British Home Counties at a rate of more than a hundred a day, killing thousands of civilians; ballistic missiles crash into centuries-old cities. Battleships are sunk with unerring aim by a tiny number of aircraft launching guided air-to-surface missiles. Strategic bombers penetrate into the heart of enemy territory, drawing in turn fire from jet aircraft and radar-equipped night-fighters. Submarines range under the oceans, attacking the enemy without ever having to emerge out of the waters; equipped with ballistic missiles, they can wreak terror in their adversary's heartland. Robot tracked vehicles attack enemy lines or clear the way through uncharted minefields. Night-sight devices make round-the-clock military operations possible. Modern electronics give military commanders the ability to detect their adversaries and orchestrate their own actions in real time, that is without the slightest delay between a decision and its implementation.

Déjà Vu All Over Again
This is not a capsule description of the Gulf War, and its whizz-bang technology, but a schematic reminder of the closing stages of the Second World War. More than 32,000 cruise missiles (German V-1s) were manufactured, of which 9,200 were launched during a period of four months in 1944 against the UK, where they killed close to 5,000

civilians. Some 4,300 ballistic V-2s (comparable to today's Scud missiles) were launched by Germany over an eight-month period. Radio-controlled 'I 400 FX' air-launched missiles destroyed, *inter alia*, the Italian battleship *Roma* in 1943. US and British long-range bombers ravaged Germany, opposed by its Messerschmitt Me-262 jet aircraft and radar-guided night-fighters. Long-range German snorkel submarines were deployed at the end of the war, which also witnessed initial development work on underwater-launched ballistic missiles. Remotely guided unmanned Goliath mini-tanks were used by the Germans during the last two years of the war. The first infra-red devices were used against Soviet tanks during night-time operations in January 1945. The strategic and tactical use of radio communications and the decisive use of radar during the Second World War, not least in the Battle of Britain, are familiar to all.

Even such a bare-bones description highlights one of the paradoxes of the current situation. Much of what passes today for hi-tech is a straightforward extrapolation of long-standing developments. Furthermore, 'new' technology can take many years to reach its full potential as an effective part of an operational force structure. Thus it took several decades to move from the invention of battle tanks (1915) to their effective use in the *Blitzkrieg* (1939–40). This viscosity in introducing new technology is increased by the long lifetimes of the tools of war, when they are not expended in battle. Aircraft and warships can serve for decades provided they are periodically retrofitted with the latest electronic kit and upgraded with new armaments. For example, the B-52 strategic bomber entered service during the 1950s; the US Air Force plans to keep a substantial number operational until 2040.

The Revolution in Military Affairs

What meets the eye is not necessarily the most important. A number of fundamental but initially unspectacular technological breakthroughs have taken place in recent years, leading to increasingly revolutionary applications.

At the top of the list, because it lies at the technical and organizational heart of the current revolution in military affairs, is the invention of the semiconductor, with its first and, by today's standards, primitive manifestation as the transistor in 1948. Followed by the first integrated circuits (1958) and microprocessors (1971), it has benefited from continuous quantitative improvement, with the processing capability for a given surface of silicon multiplying more than fivefold every five years. This means that, in the forty years which have elapsed since the first integrated circuits, capacity has increased by close to nine powers of five, or more than a millionfold, on the basis of unchanged cost and size. If such a trend had prevailed in the automobile industry, an ordinary car would cost around £4 and would run 100,000 kilometres on a litre of petrol.

In practical terms, this makes it possible to transform the 'silliest' of munitions – such as 500lb iron bombs which have hitherto relied on the laws of gravity and air resistance for determining their landing point after being dropped from their aircraft – into a 'brilliant' weapon. Such a bomb can have an ever cheaper guidance package strapped on, which will help steer it towards its target.

These trends are set to last well into the new century. Eventually, physical barriers will be met in microelectronics, with the size of individual atoms possibly setting those limits, but this point is still far from being reached. If today's laptop computer has more computing power than the world's largest room-sized computer had in the mid-1950s, in the near future the power of that PC will fit into a single chip. For the human user, the limiting factor to miniaturization will be the size of the display screen. This will not be a consideration on board inanimate weapons systems into which ever greater amounts of processing power will be crammed.

Alongside the military consequences of the electronics and information revolution several technical breakthroughs are occurring, with more or less portentous consequences, in the fields of stealth, lasers and biotechnology.

Stealth, the art of making weapons almost invisible to the enemy, is the most recent and hi-tech version of camouflage and concealment. Metal and traditional forms and structures are abandoned in favour of 'low observable' paints, composite materials, shapes and structures. A two-metre missile can be given the radar cross-section of a playground marble. In contradistinction to modern electronics and software, where progress is driven by the general requirements of society, stealth is a purely military technology: civilian air-traffic controllers are interested in making airliners more, rather than less, visible. Stealth is expensive when it is applied to large and complex objects such as combat aircraft: it has cost the United States $45 billion since its inception to develop and produce twenty stealth B-2 strategic bombers. However, it becomes more generally affordable when applied to smaller devices such as missiles.

When the principle of lasers, using light (or other wavelengths, such as infra-red or ultra-violet) for projecting and directing energy, was discovered in 1958, it was thought that they might play the role of 'death rays' *à la* Flash Gordon. Lasers have captured imaginations – as in the cinematic *Star Wars* trilogy – and research budgets. Indeed, they have already proved to be of military importance in non-lethal applications, for communications, guidance, range-finding and gun-laying purposes. Although much American money and effort has been put, and continues to be put, into research for lasers which can shoot down rockets from the ground or the air, no such systems have yet reached the battlefield. This may change, but problems remain. To be militarily effective, lasers must shoot off large amounts of energy at their targets in short bursts. This entails access to a bulky and potentially vulnerable power-plant. Lasers also have great trouble coping with the normal turbulence of the atmosphere. Further progress in electronics, with computing power compensating in real time for some of these effects, may be part of the answer.

Biotechnology may become a major factor in the military arena. No doubt biological and chemical weapons are as old as war itself: poisoning wells, or polluting besieged towns with the carcasses of diseased animals were biblical or medieval forerunners of the widespread use of chemical weapons during the First World War or the Iran–Iraq War of 1980–8. Although their battlefield effects were unpleasant, chemical weapons did not determine the outcome of these conflicts. However, the accidental death of 6,954 people caused by the leakage of an American chemical plant in Bhopal, India, in 1984 is an indication of the destructive potential of some modern chemicals, even in the absence of any military intent. A Japanese religious sect, Aum Shinrikyo, was able to produce nerve gas and to proceed with field tests in both Australia and Japan without being detected. In March 1995, this gas was used against travellers in the Tokyo area mass transit system, killing twelve and injuring more than 5,000. The same sect had also initiated research into biological weapons.

The future picture is particularly grim in the area of biological weapons. Since the 1980s, Iraq has produced large quantities of particularly noxious microbes, which were thankfully not used during the Gulf War. Iraqi-produced botulism, aflatoxin and anthrax could have produced serious casualties among coalition soldiers. The military threat was real enough, since we now know that by the time of the Gulf War some 165 bombs containing such germs had been produced for delivery by Iraqi aircraft, as well as twenty-five Scud warheads.

Even more ominously, biotechnology has now opened up the prospect of modifying the genes of micro-organisms in order to create new strains of disease or to produce poisons against which there exists no vaccine or antidote. This is the hideous face of techniques which have been harnessed to produce life-saving substances such as interferon or insulin. Unfortunately, this is a realm which will be extraordinarily difficult to control. Although the technology implies specialized know-how and equipment in the medical and biological fields, it does not require a broad and diversified industrial base; nor is it immensely expensive. Fairly small facilities can suffice, and their products can be transported in containers which cannot be readily detected.

There have also been improvements of existing technologies. Satellites for military purposes and smart weapons offer dramatic examples of this. Every part of the Earth can be observed by spy satellites, picking up levels of detail sufficiently small to target a weapon at the right-hand window of a house rather than at the left-hand one. Not only is this within the technical reach of the United States and the erstwhile Soviet Union; France and Israel have also joined the game, as will others. Costs too, which used to be considerable in this area – billions of dollars for US Keyhole satellites which can see objects less than a few dozen centimetres across – are beginning to come down, thanks to the overall progress of information technology. By the end of the decade, spy satellites will be available for a few dozen million dollars, well within the grasp of small states and large corporations; these satellites will be to Keyhole what a Citroën 2cv is to a Rolls Royce. But just as a Citroën 2cv will get one from A to B, cheap spy satellites can have the same high resolution as some of their costlier cousins. The information gathered by these devices can be factored at ever lower costs into the 'intelligence' of 'brilliant weapons'; smart weapons will be assigned their targets in close to real time thanks to data acquired by satellites and other sources of intelligence.

The development of cheap and accurate equipment for locating oneself and one's target is of similar strategic importance. In less than ten years, the US Global Positioning System (GPS), consisting of twenty-four satellites, has made it possible to navigate with an accuracy of a few metres to several dozen metres. This system is complemented by a similar Russian network, GLONASS. GPS is rapidly becoming indispensable for society as a whole: it is, for instance, beginning to replace traditional air-traffic control as a means of regulating the movements of airliners. Thus the US or Russia won't have the option of simply shutting off their satellites in case of war. The practical consequence is that any country acquiring even rudimentary cruise missiles can give them pinpoint accuracy for a ridiculously low cost. Can one imagine the military effect of German V-1 'buzz bombs' in 1944 having better than ten-metre precision rather than the erratic ten-kilometre inaccuracy they actually possessed? In such a contingency, the Allies would have been compelled to evacuate the D-Day landing beaches in Normandy.

Smart weapons – highly accurate, low-cost weapons tied into lower-cost, higher-quality intelligence-gathering and command-and-control arrangements – are characteristic of the cutting edge of war tomorrow. The technology is advancing fast and is, in turn, being pushed forward by strategic pressures. Now that the Soviet Empire is gone,

NATO's countries are no longer threatened by territorial invasion, which means that whatever military activity they engage in will usually be about strategic rather than life-or-death interests. The Gulf War and the Bosnian conflict are examples of this.

Under such circumstances, a high premium will be given to reduction of losses, whether they be our own or those of the innocent bystanders of the theatres in which we intervene. This calls for the ability to launch unmanned weapons from afar – what is called 'stand-off' capability – such as long-range cruise missiles. In the same spirit, new systems will operate against an enemy without direct human intervention, including 'arsenal ships' containing up to several hundred ready-to-launch cruise missiles, pilotless aircraft or, on the battlefield, driverless vehicles whose sensors and computing power allow them to find their own way. In some cases, such robot devices will be barely visible to the naked eye, thanks to the progress of 'nano-engines', the marriage of microelectronics with mechanics. Smart weapons will be endowed with great discrimination and accuracy in dealing with their chosen targets, the product of excellent real-time intelligence and high-precision terminal guidance, in order to avoid what is euphemistically described as 'collateral damage' – in plainer language, the unintended butchering of civilians or the gratuitous destruction of militarily irrelevant assets.

The thrust of this revolution in military affairs is reinforced by budgetary pressures. Unmanned missiles or satellites packed with electronics escape what has been called Augustine's Law, popularized by Norman Augustine, the redoubtable defence official and businessman who heads the world's largest defence contractor, Lockheed Martin. In essence, this states that the cost of major weapon platforms – combat aircraft, main battle tanks, aircraft carriers and the like – doubles with each change of generation. Thus the point has been reached where certain weapon platforms have simply become too costly to purchase. When Augustine's law was coined during the Cold War, the forecast outcome was that by 2021 the US Air Force would be able to purchase only one state-of-the-art manned combat aircraft a year. Given post-Cold War budget cuts, this stage may be reached rather earlier. In addition, when a single platform costs as much as it does – for instance, more than $2 billion for a single American B-2 bomber, more than $10 billion for a fully equipped nuclear-powered French aircraft carrier – the consequences of losing it act as a major incentive to keep it out of harm's way, which rather reduces its military utility.

Hence, the structure of the armed forces will have to change. The force structures inherited from the Cold War are those of a muscle-bound athlete: too strong to cope with contingencies calling for nimbleness in contests where the issue is not national survival. In a limited but real shooting war, the weapons of choice will not be extraordinarily costly platforms, but stand-off systems, such as cruise missiles or pilotless aircraft. In turn, stand-off weapons can be launched from fairly low-cost platforms kept well to the rear: arsenal ships at sea, retrofitted old combat aircraft, or even militarized airliners.

Budget pressure also increases the emphasis on electronics and computing power brought from the general economy, where the discipline of flat-out competition in the marketplace promotes cost reduction along with excellence of performance. The defence sector will rely less and less on so-called military specifications, which imply custom-built and therefore costly components and subsystems. This is in contrast to the previous decades of the century, in which military requirements tended to generate spin-off towards the general economy. The first jet aircraft, the first computers and the ancestor of the Internet were all developed to meet military needs. Internet, initially called ARPAnet – after the name of the American Defense Advanced Research Projects Agency – was set up by the Pentagon in 1969. It was to serve not only as a modern means of communication between scientists and engineers working on military contracts, but also as part of an effort to maintain connections between US research establishments even after a Soviet nuclear attack would have destroyed traditional communication links. But if the Internet was a child of the Cold War, the hyperactive civilian adolescent it has since become will, in turn, spawn military applications in future command and information systems.

This new reliance of defence on the civilian sector has major strategic consequences, since anyone with a minimum of financial means and technical expertise at their disposal will have access to the fruits of the process. The days when it could be said, as in the era of colonial conquest, that the Western countries would prevail because 'we have the Maxim gun and they do not' are rapidly passing and the old industrial countries will find that their technical advance in military affairs is a wasting asset.

Video-Clip Wars

Technology will also change war as it is fought out through the media. War being a battle of wills, its propaganda and information dimension has always been important, as is made clear in the first recorded accounts of conflict in the Bible Lands, Ancient Greece or the China of the Warring Kingdoms. Technology which offers the instantaneous relay of breaking news – and, just as important, the expectation of instant coverage – has now become a reality.

Live or close-to-real-time TV coverage offers extraordinary opportunities for contenders in the battle of the wills. The crude bomb that exploded during the 1996 Olympic Games in Atlanta enjoyed a degree of international coverage out of all proportion to its casualties or political significance. The visual from the Atlanta open-air entertainment park – which drove out coverage of the unexplained mid-air explosion of flight TWA 800 off the US coast a few days earlier – was a vivid example of the inflationary impact of pent-up demand among journalists and viewers for news that seemed in short supply. Instant access and demand for it will become more widespread in the coming decades, as cheaper and more convenient satellite transmission from camera in the field to television set in the living room becomes available and as the use of on-line computer networks spreads.

Spectacular changes indeed, but to what extent will they really transform the manner in which wars are fought, notably by open democracies? A first key lies in the fact that real-time and almost universal media coverage does not necessarily entail the disappearance of censorship or manipulation. Indeed, the opposite may be the case: in a civilization which becomes accustomed to quick access to news, what will count for the broadcaster is the existence of immediately available images as opposed to access to higher-grade but less spectacular and less rapidly available information. The probing war correspondents who bedevilled the lives of field commanders from Balaclava (1854) to the fall of Saigon (1975) are not nearly as valuable to the shareholders of the modern broadcasting media as exciting live imagery hyped up by talking heads.

This reality has been rapidly seized upon by the military and their political masters, since it provides the opportunity for exercising new forms of control on the flow of news from battlefield to living room. The Gulf War showed what could be done, following the smaller-scale experiment conducted by the US military during the invasion of Grenada in 1983. In the Gulf, journalists were cooped up in rear-echelon hotels, occasionally taken on brief, highly regimented tours of the forces well clear of the front lines, and fed with whatever could produce good television. Militarily trivial but otherwise lively information was pumped through the system: video-game images from smart bombs; fireworks as incoming Scuds were met by Patriot surface-to-air missiles; Multiple-Launch Rocket Systems (MLRS) generating plumes of smoke as they blasted away towards Iraqi lines beyond the horizon . . . There was hardly any access to the front itself. Not a single dead Allied soldier was ever shown during the war itself.

The pace of coverage has now become that of the video-clip: staccato reporting, in a context where one item of news immediately chases away the previous one, and where the presentation of information becomes an element of audience entertainment in competition with other forms of entertainment. Under those circumstances, coverage of military intervention in conflicts of less than vital importance has to be self-contained – in effect, a story with a beginning and an end – and it has to be dramatic, as well as positive, since only those characteristics will sustain both audience interest and political support. The Gulf War had to be short in its 'active' phase, even if its build-up could be slow, since the preparatory phase could be dealt with as the deliberate setting of the stage for the ensuing drama.

This means that two types of war not involving vital interests will be sustainable in a modern society: on the one hand, short and apparently decisive conflicts with a high media profile; on the other, long-drawn-out affairs provided they retain a low degree of media interest, which in turn implies an absence of casualties or other unpleasantness. US forces could remain in Beirut for fourteen months from September 1982 because nobody really noticed, once the hoopla surrounding the initial deployment had died down. As soon as spectacular casualties occurred – the truck-bombing of the US headquarters in Beirut in November 1983 – the cue for the exit was given.

With the development of access to the media – we can call it mediatization – these effects will become ever more pervasive. Iran, Saudi Arabia or China seek in vain to suppress satellite dishes for private use; and yet these are prominent fixtures compared with the unobtrusive means of access to the Internet or to the global direct satellite mobile telephone networks which will proliferate during the coming decade. This extreme mediatization of conflict will play into the hands of groups conducting terrorist operations or countries undertaking a high-prestige *coup de main*: either the targeted party will have to resolve the conflict in its favour immediately, or it will have to give in.

This comes with a caveat: the logic of mediatization can go into reverse when the challenged entity considers that its vital interests are at stake. As we have noted, if damage is inflicted against forces or assets engaged in the defence of peripheral interests, the media pressure will tend to play against continuing a military operation. This is what happened to the Americans in Beirut in 1983. But if a given society feels that its essential interests – territorial integrity, political freedom, national sovereignty and the like – are being threatened, the media can help sustain patriotic fervour for the long haul. In such situations, even bad news – the Japanese attack on the US fleet at Pearl Harbor, for instance – will become part of the process of mass mobilization.

Chapter 2
The Devil's Playground

During the Cold War, the opposition between the Soviet Empire and the West was, with few exceptions, the shaping force of the world's military conflicts. Admittedly, most wars had their own unique origins: it didn't take a KGB plot or a CIA conspiracy to set Arabs and Israelis at each other's throats. But scarcely any conflict, including the Arab–Israeli wars, evolved independently of superpower intervention. On the one hand, each of the superpowers was prone to provoking, fuelling or exploiting conflict to its own ends, if only for fear that its rival would seize an advantage. This increased the number and lethality of conflicts which otherwise would either not have happened or would at least have remained of a lower order of intensity. The wars in Korea and Vietnam are cases in point. On the other hand, after the Cuban Missile Crisis of 1962, neither of the superpowers wished to put to the ultimate test the limits of their mutual nuclear deterrence. So-called regional conflicts were not allowed to get out of hand. The October 1973 war pitting Israel against Egypt and Syria was an example of this mixture of superpower 'arson' (in the form of massive airlifts of weaponry by the US and the USSR to their respective allies) and 'fire-fighting' (the same superpowers imposing a ceasefire).

The Cold War, with its emphasis on security, helped create a sense of willing discipline among the democracies; and among other states it provided an excuse for repressive political systems. In the field of warfare, as in others, the disciplines of the Cold War system have disappeared. This is often for the good. The removal of the threat of a nuclear holocaust as a result of a superpower confrontation is not a small blessing. There is also a lot to be said for the disappearance of conflicts which relied heavily on superpower and other outside support – the return to peace in Southern Africa, in Ethiopia–Eritrea, in Indo-China, in Central America, owes a lot to the passing of the Cold War. But the end of the ideological and power contest between the USSR and the USA has also opened new opportunities for warfare. Liberation from Soviet oppression and from the threat of a third world war has produced many beneficiaries, some worthy, some much less so. War has also been freed, from the particular rules and occasional limits set by the realities of the Cold War. Former 'no-go areas' have been opened to warfare, from the Balkans to Tajikistan. Formerly important allies or assets have ceased to be regarded as worth having. State power has been allowed to break down in areas considered to be marginal to global prosperity, such as Africa. Unrestrained violence has occurred as a result, notably producing disintegration in Somalia and Liberia.

The age when the West and the East had to some extent to see every conflict through the prism of the superpower confrontation has given way to a period of stand-alone rationales for warfare. During the next twenty-five years we may in effect witness four broad categories of warfare. First, there will be 'rogue state' wars, undertaken by virulently anti-Western dictatorships gaining access to weapons of mass destruction. This type of conflict is most likely to occur in the 'crescent of crisis' extending from North Africa to Afghanistan. Although a source of widespread anxiety, this may not prove to be the most difficult challenge to cope with. The second category will be wars of secession by sub-groups seeking power for themselves within previously existing states, as in the former Yugoslavia.

The Indian subcontinent and subSaharan Africa, as well as the Balkans and parts of the former Soviet Union, are likely theatres of such conflicts, which may be characterized by extremes of hatred and violence. Third will be wars of disruption directed by foreign and domestic groups against the functioning of existing societies, with means as different as the terror of extreme violence or the 'virtual destruction' of cyberwar. The industrialized countries will be particularly vulnerable to this type of warfare. Finally, there will be 'classical' Clausewitzian wars, where nineteenth-century goals will be sought with twenty-first century tools, East Asia being particularly at risk. If much of the world has been witnessing a reduction of the role of the nation-state as the prime actor in foreign affairs and as the monopoly wielder of the power to make war, these changes have not occurred in East Asia. There, traditional state-based power relations are the norm. On the basis of current trends, in 2014 East Asia may bear an uncanny resemblance to 1914 Europe.

These categories of warfare will rarely be encountered in a 'pure' form – for instance, the Gulf War fits into at least three of these categories – and they can be waged with widely varying degrees of violence. But, for the purpose of highlighting the stakes and the risks involved, we will illustrate these various types of war with capsule scenarios with a mix of regional conflicts and confrontations involving the remaining superpower, the United States; these scenarios also assume high levels of force, thus putting into play an array of tools in keeping with the nature of the conflict described.

Rogue State: How Libya Returned to the Stone Age
In 2012, Colonel Muammar Gadaffi celebrated his seventieth birthday with a great military parade and a grand display of fireworks on the Tripoli waterfront. Although

invitations had been sent to the heads of state in countries belonging to what used to be called the Third World, only two of his peers stood at his side on the reviewing stand: Fidel Castro (age eighty-five) of Cuba and Saddam Hussein (age seventy-five) of Iraq. His other anti-imperialist friends had died away or been overthrown. Gadaffi knew that he was himself a dying man, his personal physician having diagnosed the onset of Creutzfeldt-Jakob disease.

Despite its oil exports, Colonel Gadaffi's police-state was a wreck of a country, after forty years of economic mismanagement. Neighbouring Tunisia, a fraction of the size of Libya, had meanwhile become the first of the 'Lions' – African and Arab states which had followed in the footsteps of the Asian Tiger economies. But Gadaffi had something that his neighbours didn't. After many years of frustrating efforts, Libya had assembled a handful of missile-launched nuclear warheads and weaponized nerve gas and biotoxins.

In 2012, the day after the birthday parade, the Libyans used the old trick of staging manoeuvres as a cover for the invasion of Tunisia. After claims that there had been Tunisian armed provocations, Libyan ground forces crossed the border. Radio Tripoli called for an immediate Tunisian capitulation, otherwise 'special weapons' would be used. Conversely, Tunisian acquiescence would bring about the merger of the two states. Although Tunisian forces were unprepared, they managed to hold their ground a hundred kilometres or so to the rear of the border along the Mareth Line of Second World War fame. Washington and Paris had immediately declared their readiness to provide full political and military support, an offer snapped up by Tunis. Forty-eight hours after the Libyans had entered Tunisia, the conflict was internationalized.

Libya took the first step in changing the nature of a war

which had started out as a remake of El Alamein rather than of *Star Wars*. Colonel Gadaffi loosed a barrage of eighteen Scud missiles against Tunis and Bizerte. Many of these antiquated devices broke up in flight and crashed harmlessly into the neighbouring waters or on to farmland. However, five chemical and three biological warheads scored bull's-eyes and successfully dispersed their deadly cargo in heavily populated central Tunis. Fifty thousand inhabitants were killed by nerve gas. Within days several hundred thousand more were in the terminal throes of lethal anthrax.

The Western Allies' military intervention was at once thrown into high gear. Within minutes of the Libyan Scud strike, swarms of precision-guided bombs and cruise missiles destroyed the bulk of Libya's military communication and command networks, along with most of the air-defence and logistics infrastructure. The Allies succeeded in doing what the Gulf War coalition had signally failed to do in 1991 despite their overwhelming airpower: to detect and destroy mobile Scud launchers. Within twenty-four hours, Libya was shorn of most of the means of waging an organized war, whether offensive or defensive. A US Marine brigade and a French combat helicopter regiment were deployed alongside their Tunisian allies in the next few days.

Each Allied infantry soldier was equipped with a glove-back computer screen allowing him (or her) to visualize any chosen aspect of the battle, providing instant 'battle-field awareness'. Hand-held keyboards enabled soldiers to call in support, exchange information or keep in touch with battlefield 'crawlies' – miniature robots operating behind Libyan lines, providing data or wreaking electronic havoc. Head-up displays mounted on goggles no more obtrusive than ordinary spectacles made it possible to 'see' in the infra-red and ultra-violet parts of the spectrum – a useful capability for operating at night or for detecting camouflaged sources of heat such as tank engines or bivouacs.

This select force, operating against ten times its own number, reached and breached the Libyan border within hours of its deployment. However, when it approached the outskirts of Tripoli, Colonel Gadaffi played his last card, issuing an ultimatum: either the foreign forces returned from where they came, or else Libyan nuclear weapons would be detonated. Relayed by the Libyan leader himself during an interview by Oriana Fallaci on CNN, the threat could not be disregarded. Gadaffi was helped by the elements. A major thunderstorm, preceded by a sandstorm, struck in the Tripoli area. Smothered by the sand, soaked by the rain, the Allies forces were temporarily pinned down, their precision-guided weapons blinded by the elements while the electrical storm played havoc with their computer links. For a time, combat conditions were brought back to those of an earlier age.

Allied forces were ordered by their political leaders to cease fire and stop their advance, while Gadaffi was put on notice that any use of weapons of mass destruction against the Allies would be punished in kind, and disproportionately so.

Had Gadaffi been a healthy and sane dictator, mutual deterrence of sorts could have taken hold. He would have avoided running the mortal risk of putting Allied determination to the test, and would thus have remained in power, albeit in charge of a shattered country partly occupied by the enemy. As an already condemned man, he decided otherwise. His remaining mobile missile launchers were wheeled out and fired at the main US and French staging-point. The four Scuds and six surface-to-surface cruise missiles were intercepted by American missile defences. Two nuclear warheads, however, made it through the defences. The bombs wrought less damage than the previous chemical and biological attacks against Tunisia, because the Allied forces were well spread out in the desert: immediate casualties were in the low thousands. But the Allies did not wait to count the bodies. Retaliation was massive. Within minutes, two multiple-warhead Trident II D-5 missiles were launched by the submarine USS *Tennessee* and the French shot ten ASMP-*Plus* nuclear cruise missiles from their Corsica-based *Rafale* fighter-bombers. The combined twenty-six warheads erased Tripoli and Benghazi from the face of the earth and destroyed Libya's hitherto untouched petroleum industry. Along with its dictator, Libya had ceased to exist as a nation.

Secession: The Break-Up of India

By 2010, successful economic reform had transformed a hitherto slow-growing Indian Union into the new Asian powerhouse: ten years of 10 per cent growth a year had turned India with its then 1.1 billion inhabitants into the equivalent of what China had become in the mid-1990s. However, and unlike the Chinese heartland with its fairly homogeneous population, India was composed of a disparate patchwork of ethnic, linguistic and religious groups and castes. Over time, unequal economic growth created unbearable strains between the successful states of the Union – from the flourishing agro-business of Punjab to the world's software capital in Bangalore via the booming financial centre of Bombay – and those which were left behind – the teeming unemployed and destitute masses of states such as Uttar Pradesh and Bihar. The richer states became increasingly resentful of the financial demands of the All-Union authorities in favour of the underprivileged, who were increasingly being mobilized by a national-populist surge of militant Hindu xenophobia.

After the electoral victory of the Hindu nationalists at

the Union level, Karnataka's 60 million inhabitants issued a unilateral declaration of independence, followed by Maharashtra (100 million) and Bengal (90 million). Comparatively small but economically powerful Punjab split into a three-way civil war between Sikh separatists, central government forces and local Hindu authorities. In major Indian cities, lynch mobs attacked those belonging to the 'wrong' group. Organized warfare erupted between federal forces and local militias initially equipped through the seizure of isolated garrisons, arms depots and deserting Union units. The conflict rapidly escalated as the arms industries in the hands of the secessionists were made to operate at maximum capacity; modern combat aircraft, missiles, main-battle tanks and artillery were fielded by all sides. The software wizards of Bangalore wrought electronic havoc in the Union forces' command-and-control system.

The ethnic fragility of the Union was paralleled by the geographical and political dispersal of territorially unconnected but individually powerful secessionist areas, making for a particularly violent conflict, reminiscent – albeit on a vastly larger scale – of the American Civil War of 1861–5 or the Spanish Civil War of 1936–9. The strategic stakes could not be ignored by China, Russia and the United States, but the general tendency of the outside powers was to keep their distance from a conflict with an unpredictable outcome. Although sorely tempted to seize Kashmir frmo a beleaguered Delhi government, Pakistan too stayed out of the conflict.

The most vulnerable secessionist state, Maharashtra, escalated the conflict by using biologically produced neurotoxins against the federal forces. Flying columns of Maharashtra and Bengali soldiers then converged on New Delhi. As a last resort, the Union threatened the use of nuclear weapons. Maharashtra, having seized weapons-grade plutonium from the atomic reprocessing facility in

Trombay, threatened retaliation in kind. Stalemate and a ceasefire appeared to be within grasp. But the progress of a particularly effective computer virus created a panic among Union authorities, who feared the rapid crippling of their capability to exercise effective command and control of their nuclear weapons. Faced with a 'use them or lose them' dilemma, the federal government fired a salvo of nuclear-tipped Prithvi ballistic missiles against secessionist targets.

The nuclear exchange destroyed key cities and infrastructure in the former Indian Union, killing millions. But a third world war did not take place, because outside powers stood aloof from the internecine massacre. Nor did this crossing of the nuclear threshold lead to a 'nuclear-winter', plunging the planet into a new Ice Age: after all, the quantity of nuclear weapons actually used remained significantly smaller than the dozens of much more powerful nuclear tests which had been conducted in the atmosphere each year by the superpowers in the early 1960s. However, the world economy was precipitated into a devastating economic brief but depression as the nuclear scare paralysed consumers and investors everywhere.

On the ground nothing was resolved in the short run, large scale military operations being impossible to conduct under such conditions: anarchy prevailed for the better part of the decade.

War in Cyberspace: An Electronic Pearl Harbor

As the end of the millennium approached, new sects and fringe groups emerged in a United States more than ever characterized by religious revivalism and extreme individualism. Among such organizations, the Brigade of Luddites Against State Terror (BLAST) was to acquire a particular notoriety for having unleashed what the then serving American President was to call a 'micro-second that will live in infamy'. BLAST had recruited a phalanx of science students from prestigious universities, building on the organizational expertise of some of the most skilled people in the death-and-terror business. The creed of the group was simple: the world would come to an end on 1 January 2000. Only the select few would gain redemption, having actively helped the Lord bring about the end of a World of Evil exemplified by the oppressive federal American state.

The battle plan of the sect consisted in the injection of an unobtrusive dormant computer virus into the software of the main ground-based US telecommunication nodes. The virus would be activated as soon as the digits 00 had replaced the digits 99, a threshold which would be crossed at midnight on 31 December 1999 upon the arrival of the new millennium. Once set in motion in cyberspace, the virus would comprehensively destroy the software of all digital telephone switching equipment. Its effectiveness would be enhanced by the frailness of computer systems which would have trouble enough coping with the normal passage from 1999 to 2000.

At 00:00 on 1 January 2000, North America's main telecommunications networks went dead; voice and data links were interrupted. The Millennium Virus brought the US economy to an instant halt, as all externally networked organizations, from financial markets to mail-order firms, were prevented from communicating. CB operators, ham radio buffs and subscribers to the first satellite systems offering direct communications links were among the select groups which could still talk, albeit only with others similarly equipped. A number of defence facilities with their inward-focused networks, strong electronic 'firewalls' and dedicated communication links could still function normally. But these were the exceptions.

Across the country, airports closed – indeed two airliners collided in mid-air, killing hundreds, as a result of air-traffic-control failure. Hospitals with their computers down were operating in battlefield conditions. A cataclysm was only narrowly averted when an overflow of liquefied natural gas occurred in Boston Harbor because of the electronic failure of valve-control equipment during transshipment operations.

Fortunately the US was not at war; and the economy would hardly have been functioning anyway on 1 January 2000. The great American talent for organization helped limit the initial catastrophe; indeed, after a few months of economic collapse and its toll on the standard of living, a new boom began, led by firms specializing in hardened software, in 'firewall' technology protecting computer networks, and in satellite-based voice and data links. Constellations of satellites entirely obviating the need for earth-based relays and switches spread like wildfire.

Unlike the Japanese during the surprise attack on Pearl Harbor, the cyberterrorists remained undetected after their misdeed. Soon they were busily working on the algorithms for Satellite Array Destruction, which became known as the SAD Virus, to be used on the 150th anniversary of the death of Ada Byron in 1851. Ada Byron, a daughter of Lord Byron, could be described as the first computer programmer, who had provided the software for Babbage's mechanical calculator, the forerunner of the digital revolution.

Wars of Value Projection, or How the US Navy Was Sunk

Before the post-Cold War era had entered its second decade, hopes of establishing a 'new world order' had been reduced to proportions rather more modest than those expressed by President Bush during the Gulf crisis of 1990–1. In Iraq as in Bosnia, the incumbents had survived foreign intervention. Yet these countries had been the theatre of successful operations.

For fear of losing casualties, the United States had become increasingly wary of military interventions involving ground forces. Military operations had to aim for zero casualties. However, such stand-off interventions had fairly narrow limits against a determined foe: despite forty days of unrelenting air strikes, ground forces had to be used to secure the liberation of Kuwait in February 1991. Furthermore, these limits were to narrow further, as the corresponding technology, when available to both sides, tended to make things easier for the defender than for the intervener. This asymmetry was greatly enhanced if the intervener was aiming for a speedy and low-casualty conclusion. This is not a constraint usually experienced by the country which is being intervened against.

The US Navy was to discover this at its expense in the Battle of the Pescadores in the spring of 2007. After the reincorporation of Hong Kong into China on 1 July 1997, the leadership in Beijing sought the conquest of Taiwan. A costly but successful landing operation had captured the Taiwanese islands of Quemoy and Matsu in late 2006. A tight blockade by the Chinese air and naval forces was hampering the foreign trade on which Taiwan's economy was entirely dependent: harbours and territorial waters were mined and Taiwanese ships were sunk. However, China was careful not to attack foreign shipping on the high seas, since freedom of navigation is a vital interest of sea-faring nations, including the United States. The next step for China was to seize the Pescadore Islands, which would serve as the springboard for the final invasion of Taiwan proper, less than thirty miles distant.

Under pressure from US public opinion and the Congress, the American government decided to send a naval task force to defend the principle of self-determination in the face of military coercion. The Americans had not forgotten how Beijing had previously destroyed Hong Kong's freedom. The task force despatched to protect the Pescadores was built around the carriers *Harry S Truman* and *Dwight D. Eisenhower*, fielding a total of twenty-four F-14 and forty-two F-18 combat aircraft, along with eighty other aeroplanes and twenty-four helicopters, as well as enough Harpoon missiles to sink most of China's fleet. China was given due warning that the US force had rules of engagement which would in effect prevent Chinese forces from landing on the Pescadores. It was also pointed out to Beijing that using combat radars (by 'illuminating' prospective targets) would be considered a hostile act. This constraint was readily circumvented by the Chinese, who used their radar-surveillance satellites and their air-traffic-control radars to keep track of the US task force.

For several weeks, little happened. The Chinese fleet, after some careful probing which drew convincing American counter-moves, refrained from any behaviour which could have been construed as a threat. Indeed, it slipped away for routine repair and overhaul in Fuzhou and Amoy. Rhetoric in Beijing about 'liberation by 1 July' was all but dropped. Even the giant 'countdown-meter' which displayed the number of hours remaining before the symbolic date of 1 July was removed from Tiananmen Square. The US relaxed, while normal trade-flows with Taiwan were resumed in the wake of large and unimpeded minesweeping operations.

At twilight on May Day, the officers on watch in the *Dwight D. Eisenhower's* combat centre were intrigued by the somewhat unusual flight pattern of the regular Fuzhou–Hong Kong civilian air service, provided by a Boeing 747. Mindful of disaster caused in 1988 when the USS *Vincennes* shot down a civilian Iranian Airbus, killing 290 passengers, the task force did not respond immediately. The Americans were also hampered by the knowledge that Beijing had indicated that it also would consider the use of combat radars as a hostile act.

When US surveillance radars finally picked up the several

dozen objects released by the Boeing 747, it was too late for the American fleet to mount a convincing response; a second 'civilian' Boeing 747 flying in the first one's shadow had already followed suit. Guided by GPS as well as by infra-red and radar seekers, the swarm of cruise missiles swamped American defences. Surface-to-air missiles, Phalanx rapid-fire machine guns, decoys and smoke managed to destroy or divert up to three-quarters of the incoming rockets: but one out of four got through. The *Dwight D. Eisenhower* and the *Harry S. Truman* both took at least ten hits of armour-penetrating 800-kilo warheads. This was only the first wave; within seconds more than 200 ground-launched sea-skimming missiles followed the initial salvo. When the sun had set, the two US flagships were sinking, along with several Aegis air-defence and anti-missile cruisers, not to mention other craft. Not a single Chinese ship or combat aircraft had been damaged. Beijing sent a message through the 'hot line' to the White House that any military reprisal against Chinese territory would draw a nuclear response. To bring home the message, the doors of Chinese missile silos in Sinkiang were opened, for US spy satellites to contemplate. At the same time, China recalled that it did not consider itself to be in a state of war with the US, whose ships had no business attempting to prevent 'the settlement of a domestic Chinese matter'.

Following the Battle of the Pescadores, the United States Navy speeded up its arsenal-ship programme, which had reached prototype stage during the previous year. These barge-like ships were capable of shooting several hundred long-range cruise missiles without getting into harm's way.

Clausewitz in Asia: A 2020 Vision
The flashpoints for the 2020 War, as it later became known, were the oil and gas fields under the waters of the South China Sea. The quest for fossil fuels had become desperate

for the energy-guzzling industrialized states in the region. At the same time, these countries were seeking a geopolitical role in keeping with their recently acquired strength.

China, which had overtaken the United States economy by 2017, needed oil imports of more than 7 million barrels a day – as much as Western Europe or North America. China was also rivalling the United States in the scale of its military spending. Indonesia, with its quarter-billion population, had an economy and a military as big as Japan's. Korean reunification had reproduced the erstwhile German economic miracle. Thailand, with a population of 60 million-plus, was the economic equivalent of France. Malaysia had completed its '2020 development plan' launched in the early 1990s, and had overtaken Australia economically. All of the Asian countries were net oil importers, even Indonesia, which had been a founding member of OPEC, the Organization of Petroleum Exporting Countries.

In the late 1990s people believed that crisis had been avoided when the South-east Asian states and China had peacefully settled claims for the ownership of the Spratly Islands in the South China Sea, thought to be rich in oil. China had acquired possession of most of these tiny low-lying islands, and an international consortium had been set up between the nations of the region to share out the hydrocarbon resources. The agreement was deemed a historic breakthrough, because the matter had brought the region to the brink of war several times. Alas, it gradually transpired that the area was practically barren of oil.

Meanwhile, Indonesia struck pay dirt by discovering giant oil fields in the Natuna Island region, which had already been producing gas and oil in the early 1990s. Jakarta might have been able to benefit unhindered from the windfall: its title was strong, and its armed forces should have been capable of defending the area. But a tight-fisted Finance Ministry had prevented the establishment of a solid, in-depth defence of the oil and gas installations.

War became inevitable as the consequence of a power vacuum in Indonesia. After inconclusive election results, a coalition of opponents attempted to overthrow the government. Turmoil ensued, marked by widespread anti-Chinese pogroms in Java which inflamed emotion in Beijing. China sealed a secret alliance with Malaysia, and together they challenged the historical basis of Indonesia's possession of Natuna. Not entirely by coincidence, Chinese historians stated that the Ming Dynasty traveller and explorer Zheng He had set up an outpost in Natuna in 1433. Malaysia in turn recalled that the islands had been a favourite haunt of the pirate-princes of Sarawak. Diplomatic pressure and military moves short of war unfolded over a period of several months.

A last-ditch diplomatic conference was set up in the suitably neutral Spanish city of Algeciras to attempt to devise a solution. *En route*, the head of the Chinese delegation was assassinated by a terrorist group of the Aceh–North Sumatra Liberation Army. Beijing issued an ultimatum to the Indonesian government. The answer was considered unsatisfactory and Beijing's naval forces seized key Natuna oil installations. Most were destroyed in the process, unleashing an ecological catastrophe exceeding that created by the torching of the Kuwaiti oil wells in 1991. The modern blue-water navy which China had built up over the previous decades performed creditably in the military task of taking over the archipelago, although a number of ships were sunk by Indonesian air-launched stand-off weapons.

The 2020 War spiralled out of control as extremists took over in Malaysia. The reincorporation of Singapore into the Malaysian Federation (from which it had seceded in

1965) was a key item on their agenda but the city-state put up a robust resistance. Australia provided economic support to Indonesia. Thailand struck at Malaysia, in order to seize Kedah, Kelantan, Perlis and Terengganu, the sultanates which had been under its suzerainty before 1909 and which it had annexed for four years during the Second World War. Oil-starved Korea and Japan sought American protection.

Beijing had a relatively free hand in dealing with its southern adversaries, because the US remained studiously neutral as long as China did not attack America's interests or the territory of its allies. But fear of Russian, Japanese and Korean military involvement restrained it from committing more naval and land forces to the south than strictly necessary for achieving its limited objective of seizing and holding Natuna.

The war did not trigger the use of nuclear weapons. Beijing's nuclear arsenal deterred any strike against Chinese territory. Korea, Japan and Australia, thanks to their American alliance, had the US nuclear umbrella to shield their homelands. However, the infrastructure of all the South-east Asian states was shattered by the intensive use of air- and sea-launched stand-off missiles during the six-week war. Direct civilian casualties remained limited, since weapons of mass destruction were not used and because the geography of the area lent itself to air and naval operations rather than to the deployment of mass armies.

Indirect losses in the region were phenomenal, as starvation gripped essentially urban populations deprived of the key elements of their physical and electronic infrastructure. It would have required something like the Marshall Plan of 1947–8 to build the region to its previous dynamism and prosperity. No such plan was forthcoming. The United States of 2020 did not occupy the commanding economic position it had held at the end of the Second World War. Although Chinese, Japanese and Korean cities remained unscathed, the ecomomic disruption caused by the demise of South-East Asia as a source of consumer and investment demand led to a global slump.

Chapter 3
Grunts, Geeks and Crazies

Each generation develops its own particular organization of warfare in terms of who directs the fighting or fights the wars. The mercenary bands of the Thirty Years' War (1618–48), of which the Vatican's Swiss Guards are a residual manifestation, are one type of military organization. Armed forces as an amalgam of young noblemen and press-ganged unfortunates in eighteenth-century Europe or the *levée en masse* of the French Revolutionary Wars are other contrasting examples. They show how over fairly short periods of time the human and organizational elements of war can change.

War in the twentieth-century had two main sets of actors: conscripts and managers. Only with the draft could states raise sufficient forces to seize and hold territory against similarly organized foes. Universal and compulsory military service had been the consequence of major improvements in the organization of the central state, which made it possible to tally, induct and regiment vast cohorts of young men. This form of military organization was invented, and used with great success at the end of the eighteenth century, by a young French general, Napoleon Bonaparte, who harnessed the growing central power of the French state to new purposes. Supplying conscripts with reasonably effective weapons while providing their units with a sufficiency of long-range firepower – notably in the form of field artillery – became possible with the beginnings of mass production of standardized arms: Napoleonic artillery and musketry were early examples of this.

The other prominent member of the twentieth-century case of military characters was that of the organizer, the manager of war, in the form of the modern staff officer. Although Napoleonic warfare saw the beginnings of dedicated general staff and quartermaster organizations, these really came into their own after the middle of the nineteenth century. The Prussian General Staff had brought about within a few years of its creation the defeat of Denmark (1864), Austria and the anti-Prussian German states (1866) and France (1870–1). The German General Staff of 1871–1914 inspired other countries to follow suit, while the progress of industry, transportation networks and state organization made it possible to wage total war drawing on all of modern society's human and material resources. Over the decades, military staffs grew as the impedimenta of modern military units became ever more heavy and complex.

By the end of the Cold War, the operational aspects of staff work were playing second fiddle to logistics: in the Gulf War, millions of tonnes of material had to be moved before the first shot was fired. Any disruption of the logistics flow would have 'deorchestrated' the force build-up and disorganized the conduct of operations. It was most fortunate for the coalition forces that Saddam Hussein did not shoot one or two cruise missiles every day at the staging-points of the build-up in the port of Jubail and the airbase of Dhahran.

If General Norman Schwarzkopf is well known for having successfully directed and conducted the Allied operations in the Gulf, it is his less well-known subordinate in charge of logistics, General 'Gus' Pagonis, who made the operations possible in the first place. But this in turn brings to mind the French comment: *'C'est magnifique, mais ce n'est pas la guerre'* – it was a feat of management, not of strategy, which was accomplished. The forces of inertia such as the sheer bulk of things and people to be moved, the pressure of time, the complexity of the logistics flows, the difficulties of geography and climate: these were the defeated 'enemies'. The forces of the Gulf War coalition came very close to collapsing under their own weight. Yet there will be relatively few circumstances in which an intervention force will be able to build up a massive array without being disturbed by the real enemy.

Once one adds to that observation the political and strategic realities of the post-Cold War era, it should not come as a surprise that a substantial degree of recasting will take place as the theatre of war changes in nature. The era of the 'managers of war', in the form of military staff officers, is coming to a close, as other actors come to the fore. Three archetypes have been chosen here. They are not entirely new, but not all have played such prominent roles hitherto.

Grunts

The footsoldier will remain central to warfare. But instead of the multitudes produced by conscription from the Napoleonic Wars to the rice fields of Vietnam, the infantry-man (or woman) will have chosen his (or her) calling. Since professional armies have been around in modern industrialized countries for some time – notably in the United Kingdom and the United States – one already has a fair idea of the kind of human profile such forces tend to have.

In practice, attitudes and background do not greatly depart from what they would be in a conscript force. The percentage of ethnic minorities may be higher (as in the US Army), the proportion of working- or lower-middle-class youths may be greater (as in the British Army), than would be the case with universal military service; but the ethos and the habits are not substantially different from those prevalent in a draft army. With the partial exception of special forces – Rangers or Force Delta in the US, the Special Air Service or Special Boat Service in the UK – these professional armies do not project an image of 'dogs of war'. As for special forces, those too have their counterparts in conscript forces (the French Service Action, not to mention the Foreign Legion; the Spanish Tercio; the former Soviet Spetsnaz, and so on).

Indeed, one of the problems of professional forces in the future may be that they won't have enough of a war-fighting attitude. In modern armies, the concerns of the soldiers may not be substantially different from those of society at large: pay scales, conditions of rotation between garrisons, the state of living quarters, the situation of employed spouses and so forth may take precedence over more martial topics. In societies such as the United States which emphasize the notion of 'zero death' conflict and the need for overwhelming superiority as a prerequisite for military intervention, the notion of risk and sacrifice may become exceedingly hazy. That being said, once a military force, whether conscript or professional, has been put in the presence of a shooting adversary, little time elapses before it functions as a fighting force, if only out of a sense of active self-preservation. Its degree of success in this process will then depend on the nature and extent of prior training, tradecraft and unit cohesion.

The footsoldier – or the 'grunt' as front-line American infantrymen became known in Vietnam – of the next century will possess one major advantage and a no less important liability compared to his forebears. He, or indeed she, will benefit from the greater simplicity and ease of use which modern technology gives to modern weapons (as it does to more mundane appliances). A modern assault rifle, a GPS receiver for accurate navigation, a hand-held or glove-back computer and 'fire and forget' anti-tank missiles are immeasurably more convenient to operate, particularly in the stress of battle, than a wheel-lock musket, a compass-cum-ordnance-survey-map, a first-generation walkie-talkie or a muzzle-loading cannon. Technical sophistication goes hand in hand with simplicity of use: the difficulties of maintenance and repair are shunted towards the rear.

The liability is the immediate corollary of the asset. With such tools being made available to all and sundry, the battlefield of the future will be a particularly demanding one. With night-vision devices, the distinction between night and day will diminish; with man-portable fire-and-forget missiles and rapid-fire individual arms, attacks will occur with little opportunity to counter-fire effectively against a barely revealed foe; drones and other pilotless aircraft or robots will be on a permanent lookout and will fire (or direct fire) at any detected target; instant liaison with longer-range weapons – field artillery, combat helicopters, close-air-support aircraft – will allow the rapid and accurate concentration of heavy fire in any part of the battlefield. These conditions will force each infantry unit to spread out as much as possible in order to avoid exposing a concentration of soldiers as a target, so each individual soldier will be more on his own than ever. The modern battlefield is, in this respect, a very lonely place to be in – and the future battlefield will be even more so.

The demands of continuous high-intensity combat on each individual will be formidable, with each second implying life-or-death decision-making under extreme stress. In a sense, this will recall the round-the-clock violence of trench warfare in 1914–18 France, but on a much broader, more rapidly moving battlefield, and without the possibility of hunkering down in deep shelters during enemy artillery attacks. In the future, these will be vulnerable to all manner of precision-strike stand-off weapons. In other words, infantry clashes will either be brief, or imply the rapid rotation of soldiers in and out of the area of battle. With stand-off weapons and remotely piloted vehicles reaching deep behind the immediate ground battle area, movement in and out may itself become an arduous feat of operations and logistics. The wars of 1956, 1967 and 1973 in the Middle East or the Falklands War may be the relevant model here, with active operations lasting days or weeks rather than months or years.

In effect, short bursts of fighting will be separated by lengthier interludes of longer-range exchange of fire not involving the use of infantry, along the lines of the 1969–71 War of Attrition between Egypt and Israel after the Six Day War. Indeed, the savage character of post-Cold War army operations may make the democracies particularly wary of entering into them, unless the enemy has already had his stuffing kicked out through air and naval operations. The Gulf War offered a preview of this, with the prolonged air offensive preceding the ground attack.

Geeks

The profile of the key players in long-distance, deep-strike warfare will be largely the same as that of the people who invent new software and navigate the Internet: geeks, or nerds, who are often extremely young, libertarian and completely immersed in their world of binary digits. But if their creativeness makes the world economy move forward they will also be developing and orchestrating the most modern means of destruction.

The intelligence which they make use of will be collected by unmanned sensors: optical, radar and eavesdropping satellites, drones, remotely piloted vehicles and miniaturized, remotely operated sensors deployed in enemy-controlled territory. Strikes against fortified or heavily-defended targets will be undertaken by cruise missiles and other stand-off weapons, while area targets, such as air-fields or concentrations of vehicles, will be shattered by missiles releasing multiple bomblets. Power grids will be shorted by unmanned aircraft dispensing ribbons of metal. More insidiously, electronic networks will be infected by software-destroying viruses.

The co-ordination and management of this array of weapons will require a technical and organizational exper-tise somewhat different from what was required of the military staff officers of the First World War or the logisti-cians of the Second World War and its aftermath. Young men and women, wholly absorbed in the world of com-puter algorithms, software and networks, will be the essen-tial operators. Their outlook and background will be largely civilian, the military dimension no more than an add-on.

The comparison between video-games and modern war-fare is over-simple, but it contains more than a grain of truth. The skills for modern military mission planning are not substantially different from civilian applications, including computer games. Indeed, some of the more popular CD-ROM games are variants of declassified military mission preparation and other simulations of war. In 1996, the public could buy for $20 top-of-the-line war games which in 1993 or 1994 would have been available only to special-ized military institutions, such as the US Naval Warfare Center. The world of games is virtual, whereas hi-tech war can be real – but the software and methodology which go into them are sometimes barely distinguishable.

Crazies

'Crazies' have always been among the wielders of violence, insofar as the word applies to individuals who operate outside the mainstream rules and attitudes which prevail in a given society. These 'social suicides', inhabiting fringe groups, use extreme levels of force, while being more or less ready to accept martyrdom, but they have not usually been major actors in large-scale warfare. The *Carbonari* of early nineteenth-century Italy, the radical anarchists of a century ago in Europe, the armed terrorists of the Baby Boom generation (including *Weathermen* in the US, *Brigate Rosse* in Italy, *Rote Armee Fraktion* in Germany, *Action Directe* in France, *Cellules Communistes Combattantes* in Belgium) have all made use of violence, but no one would pretend that it was war in the habitual sense. This may change as several kinds of pressure combine.

First, a comparatively large number of individuals can fit the stereotype description of militant radicalism as their own societies lose their bearings under the strain of internal contradictions and external pressures. For instance, in much of the Islamic world, radical conduct, or rather misconduct, is all the more widespread because the societies involved remain mired in despotism or poverty while being subjected to all that is vacuous or frustrating in Western influence, and yet being denied the West's positive political and economic values. Spawning grounds for extreme radicalism have thus flourished from the Atlas Mountains to the Hindu Kush. Not all the societies involved are poor – Bahrain or Saudi Arabia are nobody's idea of Third World poorhouses – but nearly all are intolerant of political and religious dissent. Indeed, it is the few countries in the region having at least some of the appurtenances of tolerance and democracy which have proved most resistant to the emergence of widespread violent fanaticism: Morocco, Jordan, Egypt.

Second, the power of the 'crazies' to wreak violence on a large scale rises if they are backed up by the logistics of supporting states. Iran, Syria, Libya, Sudan and Iraq have, at one time or another, played this role of the 'sponsor state'. US, Saudi and Pakistani support of the Mujahidin in Soviet-occupied Afghanistan played a similar, if unintended role. 'Afghanis' – up to 15,000 terrorists from various countries trained in the refugee camps of Peshawar in Pakistan – have become a standard fixture in the Islamic world, not least in Algeria, Saudi Arabia, Egypt and even the Philippines. Although the initial US–Saudi programme has since disappeared, the infrastructure remains, with substantial support from private Gulf state sources and from some of the larger radical Islamic movements.

Last, and possibly most important, the means of terror may well become as destructive as the tools of traditional warfare. The hand-held bombs of nineteenth-century anarchists or the Kalashnikovs of the Baader–Meinhof gang (the predecessors of the Rote Armee Fraktion) could kill dozens but not thousands. Conventional explosives in car- and truck-bombs already approach the scale of military operations: 299 US and French servicemen were killed by two truck-bombs in Beirut in November 1983; 168 civilians were killed by an explosive-stuffed van in Oklahoma City in 1995. Bombs in aircraft have on several occasions snuffed out several hundred lives: 329 fatalities in the Air India flight destroyed off Ireland in 1985, and 259 in the Pan Am jet at Lockerbie in 1988. Access to weapons of mass destruction will add one or two orders of magnitude to the terrorists' ability to kill – thousands or dozens of thousands in a single attack. Given the nature of the industrial processes involved, the logistics of transportation and operational ease of use, it is more likely that biological and chemical weapons will be used, rather than nuclear explosive. A nuclear weapon is hardly simple to produce, and if acquired 'off the shelf' – something which may not be possible even in a mafiosi-infested Russia – its transportation and detonation would be complex tasks for a non-state group to conduct. A flask of viruses, toxins or nerve gas is easier to handle and use. In particular, the noisome products of the ex-Soviet Biopreparat organization are a source of concern, at least as much so as the 'loose nukes' of the former Soviet Empire.

If the recent past is any sort of guide, 'crazies' will not be lacking in knowledge or training. Unabomber, a highly skilled mathematician, or the university graduates of the Rote Armee Fraktion typify what will be a common profile. Violent radicalism demonstrates a lack of morality and common sense, but not necessarily a dearth of ability and intelligence.

Some analysts of terrorism entertain the hope that extreme groups will not use weapons of mass destruction, making the point that terrorists are more interested in being talked about than in killing for its own sake. Aside from the fact that mass murder is a sure conversation-grabber, it is more likely than not that it is the lack of capability rather than the lack of intent which has kept the numbers killed by terrorists at levels below those of more conventional warfare. Inducing fear of sudden and brutal death is the purpose of terrorism. To create that fear, the act of killing itself is not always necessary, but it is no doubt the most straightforward way of achieving that purpose.

Civilians
As in previous ages of warfare, the central characters will be playing along with that large supporting cast known as the civilian population. Its involvement has greatly varied through time. Although civilians were traditionally victim-ized by armies on the move which lived off the land – a practice which was the norm well into the Napoleonic era – states didn't have the organizational ability to field large forces for any length of time. Overall, therefore, the popu-lation at large suffered little from war outside the areas lying directly in the path of armies. Particularly savage and long-lasting conflicts with a strong religious or ideological

dimension, however, could lead to massive civilian losses: the Thirty Years' War in the seventeenth century destroyed about one-third of Germany's population.

For much of the twentieth century, civilian populations have been the principal victims of conflict, with soldiers often having a greater chance of survival than other members of the population. In 1939–45, some 50 million individuals were killed in Europe, of whom fewer than 20 million were soldiers. This pattern was repeated in many of the subsequent wars, Vietnam and Afghanistan being cases in point.

'Clean' wars, that is conflicts in which the civilian population remains essentially unscathed, have also existed in the twentieth century – most notably the series of Israeli–Arab wars of 1956, 1967 and 1973, the Indo-Pakistan wars of 1948 and 1965, and the Falklands War. It would be a mistake to ascribe the 'clean' nature of these conflicts simply to geographical factors ('there are few civilians in the desert') or to the limited nature of war aims. After all Israel and its Arab neighbours have had the means to strike at each other's population centres, including cities such as Damascus, Cairo or Tel Aviv, but have generally refrained from doing so. Nor was a conflict like the Six Day War limited in terms of its aims, since Israel's very existence was seen to be at stake by all parties at the beginning of that war. Leaving aside the restraint which the fear of reprisals can inspire, the distinction between wars of civilian slaughter and 'clean' wars depends fundamentally on whether or not the destruction or removal of civilians is in itself a war aim. The bloodiest wars are and will be those in which the answer to this question is positive. Ethnic cleansing (as in former Yugoslavia) and terrorism both arise from this wish to victimize civilians.

On the other hand, the move towards high-accuracy, long-range weaponry implies that previously unavoidable civilian (and indeed military) losses can be curtailed to a greater extent than hitherto: 'clean' wars can be made less damaging if the damage is irrelevant to the achivement of the war aims. 'Pinpoint bombing' was more often than not a bad joke during the Second World War, and numerous cities in France (for instance) bear the scars of what was then an oxymoron. Post-war US Air Force operational research came to the conclusion that some 3,000 aircraft, inflicting massive damage in the general area of the aim point, had to be used in order to guarantee the destruction of a given target the size of a football pitch. Conversely, the Gulf War demonstrated that the infrastructure of a capital city such as Baghdad could be destroyed with comparatively little damage to the surrounding people and housing.

There will thus be a greater polarization between wars directed against whole populations – Rwanda or Bosnia are illustrative of this – and wars which will in some ways resemble the fighting of the eighteenth century – military against military, with less direct impact on the population at large than was the case in the Second World War or Vietnam.

Conclusion
Choices

In warfare, as in other human endeavours, the future is not preordained. The shape of conflicts to come will be determined by initiative – individual and collective – not simply by mechanical processes dictated by technology alone. And technology itself does not evolve on its own: its manifestations and uses are the result of human decisions. So the future of war will be decided by specific choices, such as coming to terms with new weaponry, coping with terrorism or curbing the spread of nuclear weapons. In this context, the nations of America, Europe and Asia will bear an essential responsibility.

Coming to Terms with 'Smart Weapons'

There is little doubt about what technological change is bringing to the art of war. We are moving from an era marked by the massive application of indiscriminate firepower – characteristic of the wars of the Industrial Revolution – to an age where firepower can be projected from afar with great selectivity. The strategic, political and indeed moral consequences of such a shift are potentially immense.

But it remains to be seen, particularly in those countries which already possess large and well-entrenched standing armies, whether this potential will be tapped to the fullest possible extent. It may be true that 'Old soldiers never die, they only fade away'; but old armies don't even fade away – they hang on until they are blown away in a moment of truth. This is what happened to the Allied armies in the spring of 1940. High-cost equipment and practices, associated with Cold War military structures, will crowd out the lower-cost paraphernalia of the post-Cold War era. Thus a handful of state-of-the-art combat aircraft cost hundreds of millions of pounds to acquire, whereas the same sum will purchase enough cruise missiles to equip the existing air force of a major country. Most countries cannot afford both, in the same way that in the 1930s France could not afford both to extend the Maginot Line to the North Sea and build up a significant number of armoured divisions; at the end of the day, it had done neither satisfactorily, and the results were all too evident.

Unfortunately, such decisions involve complex trade-offs, the consequences of which often become apparent only in hindsight. Thus it won't be easy to choose between the priority of rapidly transporting troops afar – a reasonable proposition if most American or European wars will be fought far from home – and the priority of striking an enemy accurately with effective stand-off missiles. The first goal is immensely costly, the second much less so, but in a conflict such as the Gulf War it was not possible to do one without the other. In effect, a reduction of strategic ambitions may be the only way to reconcile the terms of such a debate. In practice, this could mean emphasizing the defence of one's own region – Western and Central Europe and its immediate vicinity in the case of the members of the European Union – as opposed to investing in longer-range power projection.

Terrorism as War, War as Terrorism

The dividing line between terrorism and warfare will be increasingly blurred. The notion of terrorism here does not embrace guerrilla warfare, which may use some of the terrorist's tools but whose actors aspire to state power and are organized in consequence. Rather, it includes the work of groups or individuals whose agendas are in complete contradiction to the eventual exercise of state power. Terror is equated in this regard with a form of social suicide. With weapons of mass destruction becoming more readily available, the scope of the destruction which such groups will be able to wreak will become less distinguishable from the destruction of war. Furthermore, since they operate from within a given society, such threats cannot be readily countered by conventional military forces or by nuclear deterrence.

In parallel, interaction between the media and society will make it increasingly appealing for some state, or state-supported, actors to use the psychology and arms of terror. The symbiosis between terrorist groups and sponsoring states (Libya, Iran, Sudan and so on) bears witness to this reality. This may well turn out to be a mistaken calculation by the countries concerned, since they will be vulnerable to the threat of reprisals against their territory and institutions in a way which would be impossible against non-state terrorists. However, much unpleasantness may occur before they are convinced of their mistake.

Prevention of and action against terrorist warfare will as a consequence become much more important than it has tended to be in the area of security and defence policy. Military forces will have to adapt to these new circumstances. Special operations commands and the forces which are subordinated to them will have to play a greater part in fighting terrorism. Specialist units and research into coping with chemical and biological weapons will have to receive a higher priority.

Circumstances certainly push the political rhetoric in such a direction. Whether it will turn into a tangible reality remains to be seen. In military organizations, as in other institutions, the scale of priorities can be measured by looking at the system of career development. The ranks attached to the corresponding special operations commands or specialist units and the career prospects opened to those who enter such forces offer tangible yardsticks of the importance being placed on the military aspects of counter-terrorism. The evidence today does not always point in that direction. This is true also of intelligence services. During the Cold War, the CIA was reputed to give the inside track to those who dealt with technical means rather than to operatives who traded in the uncertainties of 'human intelligence' – which lies at the heart of effective counter-terrorism.

Avoiding the Spread of Nuclear Weapons

The experience of the last quarter-century has demonstrated the possibility of curbing the spread of nuclear weapons beyond the small group of countries which already possess them: the five official nuclear powers (the United States, Russia, Britain, France and China) and the so-called threshold states (India, Israel and Pakistan). The tools for an effective non-proliferation policy certainly exist, and several decades of experience give a fairly clear idea of what can or should be done (or avoided) in the future.

However, things could go wrong, suddenly and dramatically. The acquisition of weapons-grade plutonium or uranium in the former USSR by so-called rogue states or terrorist groups is a possibility. So is a nuclear 'chain reaction' such as: 'North Korea goes nuclear, despite the world's efforts; South Korea follows suit (or, in a variation, a united Korea inherits the North's arsenal); Japan, given its entrenched loathing of Korea, does so in turn.' In another scenario: 'India detonates an H-bomb; Pakistan explodes an atom bomb; Iran, aided by Pakistan, has an increased motivation to become a nuclear power.' Non-proliferation is a sisyphean task, in which, at any given moment, previous progress risks being brought to naught. The good news of South Africa's denuclearization and the removal of nuclear weapons from Kazakhstan and Ukraine could thus be more than negated by subsequent developments elsewhere.

Of all policy objectives which will help avoid mass destruction, non-proliferation is possibly the most important – and this applies not only to nuclear but also to biological and chemical weapons. The international community has actually devised a remarkable treaty banning the production of chemical weapons, with an elaborate and intrusive set of verification measures. This convention came into force in 1997. Unfortunately, it is unlikely that some of the states most likely to produce and use chemical weapons – such as Libya or Iraq – will feel compelled to sign it. Similarly, the effectiveness of the international convention forbidding biological weapons – opened to signature in 1972 – is undermined by a lack of serious verification measures.

America, Europe, Asia

Some defence policy decisions are general in nature – countering terrorism, for instance, is not specific to a single region, even if the United States believed until recently in the immunity of its home ground – but others are directly tied to the strategic circumstances of a given area. America, for its part, has the ability, by virtue of its geography – no enemy state lies close to its borders – its military spending and the force structure inherited from the Cold War, to pursue several major strategic goals simultaneously, on a global scale. This inheritance, even if somewhat modified during the post-Cold War years, may prove to be a hidden liability as time passes. Under current circumstances there is little incentive for the Pentagon to focus the defence budget and organize the force structure around a small number of clear-cut priorities. Even when the Pentagon wants to reform in this way, the Congress finds reasons to impose upon it unwanted spending such as additional numbers of immensely costly B-2 stealth bombers to the detriment of less expensive post-Cold War priorities. This also applies to funding imposed by the Congress for the defence of the US against intercontinental ballistic missiles, which is arguably not the wisest way to allocate relatively scarce military spending. The armed forces themselves are often prone to over-invest in new material: it is debatable whether the US needs to simultaneously develop the F-22 combat aircraft, acquire the $200 billion Joint Strike Fighter and upgrade its existing fighter-bombers.

In 1996, the US had some 100,000 military personnel based or home-ported in East Asia and a similar number in Western Europe – a total of 15 per cent of its armed forces. These assets are essential to America's influence in the world. They also greatly facilitate far-flung US military operations, as was the case during the Gulf War. These forces stabilize the strategic situation in the regions in which they are based, reassuring local powers which would otherwise have greater cause to fear the strategic ambitions of their immediate neighbours. A US decision to reduce these overseas forces substantially would amount to an isolationist withdrawal to North America, and would lead to the opening-up of regional rivalries, notably in East Asia. The US could be tempted to carry out such reductions given the attractions of long-range stand-off weapons including strategic aircraft with cruise missiles, based in the US and capable of reaching practically any point of the globe, or arsenal ships home-ported in US waters. Such platforms with associated missiles would provide the US with 'punishment impunity' – the ability to hit anyone anywhere without serious risk to its own territory. The risk is that, as a corollary, the US would reduce its participation in expeditionary operations, such as the Gulf War, which are comparatively more risky because they imply the participation of ground forces. Occasional 'metal-on-metal' strikes by unmanned, long-range cruise missiles against air-defence installations in Iraq, of the sort which occurred in 1996, are no substitute for effective in-depth influence in the affairs of the region.

So in coming decades a US drift away from alliances and coalitions towards a combination of unilateral military action and *de facto* political isolationism is entirely possible.

The challenge of adapting forces to future risks is even greater in Europe. Europe's current defence budgets cannot bear the cost of creating a major force-projection capability. As thing stand, it is difficult enough to find a place in existing defence budgets for post-Cold War priorities in the field of intelligence-gathering (spy satellites, battlefield drones) or stand-off weaponry. Europe should concentrate on those areas which give it the greatest strategic return. Investing in intelligence, including spy satellites, is one such domain, since the better the information one has to trade, the better the terms of exchange (not least with the US) will tend to be. Similarly, it is both desirable and feasible to acquire the ability to bring significant and accurate firepower, especially in the form of stand-off weapons, to bear in the vicinity of Western Europe at relatively low cost. Such priorities would require the Europeans to retain a competent, broad-based defence industry, which in turn means that European firms should be similar in size, scope and competitiveness to those in the United States. This is entirely possible, provided European governments favour the restructuring of defence industries as much as the Americans do.

Air transport will remain a weak link in European force arrays, but it is not of the essence in dealing with threats close to home. When push comes to shove a combination of existing European air transport assets, chartering from Russian or Ukrainian airlines and American co-operation will enable contingencies further afield to be dealt with. But this is not an ideal situation, and European capabilities should at least be rationalized through pooling arrangements. Nevertheless, the weakness of Europe's air-transport capability is not a critical flaw – unless Europe wished to become a global gendarme.

East Asia, on the face of it, is in the best of situations. Rapid economic growth is generating massive new resources of which only a small proportion goes into defence. 'Modernization' rather than 'arms race' characterizes, at least for the time being, the defence policies of most of the countries in a region which is at peace – after decades of conflict and turmoil. Make profit not war appears to be the region's slogan. But this benign situation is fragile. East Asia, not to mention the Indian subcontinent, has many points in common with pre-1914 Europe: a high degree of economic interdependence, strong economic growth and the ambitions of competing powers. Numerous territorial, demographic or resource-based points of friction exist between China and many of its fifteen neighbours; and the interaction between China, Japan and Korea could prove to be as difficult to handle in the coming decades as it was at the end of the nineteenth century. The difference is that the region has become much more important for the world as a whole than it was a century ago.

The issue in Asia therefore is whether the countries of the region will create institutions and habits of mutual dialogue sufficiently strong to handle peacefully the disparate goals of its increasingly powerful states. The future of the American presence will be a key to answering that question. As long as the US remains militarily and politically engaged in the region, its influence will act as a strategic buffer, cushioning the shock of competing regional ambitions. Conversely, were the US to adopt a hands-off stance, then Asia's internecine antagonisms would be unshackled.

In the coming decades, therefore, war and peace will hinge to a major extent on American intentions and on Asia's ability to resolve its regional differences peacefully. Political decisions and hardware choices may thus combine their effects, although the former will be of more lasting significance than the latter. Warfare will be, as it has always been, the result of humanity's actions, and not a simple function of the evolution of inanimate objects, however 'smart' they may become.

Further Reading

The great classics remain indispensable, first and foremost Sun Tzu's *The Art of War*, of which there exist several translations into English (notably Oxford University Press, 1963; available in paperback), and Carl von Clausewitz's *On War* (Penguin Classics, 1982). Of more recent vintage, Thomas Schelling's *The Strategy of Conflict* (Harvard University Press, 1960); Général André Beaufre's *Introduction to Strategy* (Faber & Faber, 1965); and Lawrence Freedman's *The Evolution of Nuclear Strategy* (Macmillan, 1981) are all first class.

For a long-term view on the history of war and strategy, Sir Michael Howard's *The Lessons of History* (Oxford University Press, 1991) and Paul Kennedy's *Grand Strategies in War and Peace* (Yale University Press, 1991) are strongly recommended recent works.

For an understanding of contemporary warfare, one author's contribution stands out most strongly, that of Martin Van Creveld, who teaches at the Hebrew University in Jerusalem. Some of his more prominent books include *Supplying War: Logistics from Wallenstein to Patton* (Cambridge University Press, 1977); *Command in War* (Harvard University Press, 1985); *On Future War* (Brassey's, 1991); and *Technology and War* (Brassey's, 1991).

The Penguin Encyclopaedia of Modern Warfare (1991) is a handy compendium of facts and concepts.

PREDICTIONS

Asia and the Pacific
Climate
Cosmology
Crime and Punishment
Disease
Europe
Family
Genetic Manipulation
Great Powers
India
Liberty
Media
Men
Middle East
Mind
Moral Values
Population
Religion
Superhighways
Terrorism
Theatre
USA
Warfare
Women